If your family has been affected by a commercial truck accident, you have come to the right place. The fact that you are taking the time to educate yourself about commercial truck accidents in Texas shows that you are serious about getting a good result for your case. I hope the information in this book will help you get the best possible outcome for your truck accident case so you can move on with your life!

- David Todd

Copyright 2018 by David W. Todd. All rights reserved. No part of his book may be used or reproduced in any manner whatsoever without written permission of the author. Printed in United States of America.

Legal disclaimer: I am not allowed to give legal advice in this book. The suggestions and the warnings I provide in this book are not a substitute for consulting with or hiring an attorney. Please remember that I cannot give you legal advice unless and until you hire me and I have agreed in writing to accept your case.

Congratulations!

By ordering this book you have separated yourself from the all those truck accident victims who may wreck their truck crash injury claim because they do not know the truth about how commercial vehicle personal injury claims work in Texas. In this guide I will answer the most common questions I hear from truck accident victims and tell you some important things you should know. "**The Shocking Truth About Texas Truck Accidents**" is very unpopular among insurance companies for the trucking industry. For years they have preyed upon the ignorance of truck accident victims about their rights and how the legal process works. The insurers use this lack of knowledge to get injured Texans to give up or settle their case quickly, often for far less than the case is worth, without putting up the fight necessary to obtain full justice for their claim. By learning the information in this guide, you are taking the first step to avoid being a truck accident victim a second time and obtain the compensation you deserve.

What is the shocking truth about Texas truck accidents?

Each year in the United States, there are approximately **500,000** commercial vehicle accidents, causing **130,000** injuries and **5,000** deaths. In those wrecks **98%** of the people killed were in the passenger vehicle, not the commercial vehicle.

In Texas in 2011 there were **23,968** commercial vehicle crashes. **7,733** of those crashes caused injuries. **376** of those crashes caused **417** deaths. Of the serious crashes involving commercial motor vehicles **8%** resulted in at least one death. Only **4.7%** of those crashes that did NOT involve a commercial motor vehicle resulted in at least one death. In other words, you were almost twice as likely to die in a crash with a commercial truck such as an 18 wheeler than in a crash with another passenger vehicle!

The deadly nature of truck accidents is not as surprising once you realize **that an 18 wheeler truck can weigh up to 80,000 pounds (versus 3,000 pounds for the average passenger vehicle)** and the fact that a "big rig" tractor-trailer truck requires

one-third more room to stop. Combine these facts with the two most common causes of truck accidents, speeding and driver inattention, and you have a recipe for disaster.

The danger to those driving passenger cars exists on highways throughout Texas. The risk is particularly high in big cities like Dallas, Houston, San Antonio and Austin. When heavy trucks traveling at high speed merge with smaller vehicles in metropolitan areas the risk of accidents rises dramatically.

For example, Austin has a high number of serious injury and wrongful death truck accidents every year. As Austin has become one of the fastest-growing cities in both Texas and the entire United States, the amount of semi-truck crashes has increased rapidly. The increased traffic in Austin combined with the increased number of tractor-trailer and other types of large commercial vehicles passing through Austin on **Highway 71**, **Highway 290** and especially in the north-south corridors of **Loop 1 (MoPac Expressway)** and the **Interstate Highway I-35**, has resulted in an increase in the number of serious truck accidents in and around Austin. The statewide increase in the use of large trucks to ship goods has led to more 18 wheeler and other commercial vehicle type accidents across Texas, often resulting in serious injury or wrongful death.

What happens after a commercial truck accident in Texas?

Following a serious Texas semi-truck crash the investigating agency (Texas Department of Public Safety, local sheriff department or local police) will prepare an accident report. While useful, these reports are often inadmissible at trial because the officer does not prepare a formal accident reconstruction report or is not qualified to render an expert opinion under Texas law as to what happened.

The trucking company and its insurance company will go to work immediately after an 18 wheeler accident or other commercial vehicle crash to shift responsibility for the wreck away from the truck driver and the trucking company (and often on to the victim) to escape legal liability for a Texas truck accident.

This makes it very important to contact a lawyer as soon as possible after an 18 wheeler wreck so that they may gather evidence before it is lost or altered. Many commercial trucks have **"black box"** technology that records data about the position, speed and braking of a vehicle at the time of the accident. This data can be lost or altered if you delay contacting an attorney. Witnesses may move away or forget what they saw as time passes. Vital paperwork regarding maintenance and the mechanical history of the truck may be lost or destroyed. **If you wait to hire a truck accident lawyer, this vital case information may be lost and you may lose the ability to win your case.**

A legal claim for a Texas truck accident is complicated there are many regulations that govern truck drivers and trucking companies. A lawyer experienced in truck accident law can review your truck crash from the start with an eye towards determining what Texas or federal rules and regulations may have been violated that resulted in your accident.

Who is to blame for my Texas truck accident?

Many Texas truck accidents are caused by speeding or driver distraction. Some truck accidents are caused by equipment failure. Various parties may be responsible for causing your Texas truck accident, including the driver, the trucking company, the company that loaded the truck, the maintenance company, the truck or component manufacturer, the trailer manufacturer and the company that made the tires.

Immediately following a Texas truck accident, the insurance companies for the parties listed above will begin investigating the wreck to try and deflect blame for the accident onto someone else, even the victim. This makes it very important to discuss your case with a Texas truck accident lawyer as soon as possible following the crash so they may gather and protect the evidence you will need to show who is to blame and win your case.

What different types of commercial vehicles are involved in accidents?

18 WHEELERS

These large trucks are also known as semi-trucks, tractor-trailers or big rigs. These consist of a tractor (truck) that pulls a trailer. A trucker must have a commercial driver's license (CDL) to operate one of these vehicles. The tractor and the trailer are separate parts connected by an articulating hitch. This connection allows trucks to be easily changed between trailers. It also allows the trailer to be as large as possible while still allowing the driver to make sharp turns around corners. Some trailers are designed to be lifted directly from the road onto train cars or cargo ships. Since the trailer and tractor can move somewhat independently of each other, improper braking or steering can lead to jackknife or rollover accidents. These are the most common large trucks you have seen lined up at truck stops and moving cargo along Texas highways and they account for the majority of Texas truck accidents. Over 80% of the freight moved in the United States is moved by 18 wheelers.

EXTRA DUTY TRUCKS

These are larger rigs that carry oversized or super-heavy equipment. They may be longer or wider than a typical tractor-trailer and may require special operation permits. You may have seen these vehicles carrying houses, heavy construction parts for bridges, buildings and factories, or heavy equipment such as bulldozers.

FLATBED TRUCKS

A flatbed trailer is often used to haul items that don't fit or would be difficult to load in a typical closed "box" trailer. The items on a flatbed must be tied down and improper loading or securing of the load often leads to serious accidents.

TANKER TRUCKS

A tanker truck carries liquids which may include anything from milk to gasoline. Tanker trucks are subject to more stringent regulation if the liquid is classified as a hazardous material.

DUMP TRUCKS

Dump trucks carry sand, gravel, dirt or other loose material usually used for construction. Some dump trucks are used to haul trash to landfills. They often provide limited rear views for the driver that can lead to accidents while backing up.

What about garbage trucks?

GARBAGE TRUCK ACCIDENTS

Many people are shocked to learn that garbage trucks and dump trucks kill and injure more pedestrians per mile traveled in big cities like Austin, San Antonio, Houston and Dallas than any other type of vehicle.

Garbage trucks operate in neighborhoods where men, women and children live, drive, ride bikes and walk. Due to their design, garbage trucks have side and rear "blind spots" that can lead to tragedy when drivers do not see an adult or child in time to avoid them. There are specific rules and regulations that apply to garbage trucks. Your lawyer should find out if the garbage truck that hit you violated any of these regulations.

What about FEDEX and UPS delivery trucks?

FedEx and UPS have become two of the leading small package delivery carriers in the U.S. UPS and FEDEX have grown exponentially as the delivery service of choice for most companies selling goods online as more people order things on the internet. These delivery trucks operate in the neighborhoods of small towns throughout Texas as well as large cities like Austin, San Antonio, Dallas and Houston.

Unfortunately, the pressure to deliver packages in the least amount of time can sometimes lead to unsafe conditions for those living in the neighborhoods where UPS and FEDEX make their deliveries. Drivers who are in a hurry can sometimes forget that safety is always more important than staying on schedule.

Are tanker trucks more dangerous than regular tractor-trailers?

TANKER TRUCK WRECKS

18 wheeler accidents usually result in serious injury or death due to the huge size of the trucks involved. Tanker truck are even more dangerous since they often carry hazardous liquids that can lead to a fire or explosion during a collision. Even if the liquid does not ignite, spilling it on the road can cause passenger vehicles to lose traction and crash. In addition, liquids carried by tanker trucks make them some of the heaviest trucks on the road. This extra weight increases the risk of rollover and jackknife accidents.

Because of the dangerous nature of tanker trucks, they are subject to more regulations and insurance requirements than a standard tractor-trailer, especially if they carry hazardous liquids.

What are the most common equipment failures that cause truck wrecks?

BAD BRAKES ON BIG RIGS

It is not surprising that large commercial vehicles like semi-trucks take farther to stop than a car. An 18 wheeler truck can weigh up to 80,000 pounds versus 3,000 pounds for the average car. Despite massively powerful air-brake systems, a tractor-trailer "big rig" truck requires 33% more room to stop than a car. You do not need a Texas truck accident attorney to tell you that this makes the maintenance and adjustment of the truck brakes vital to public safety. Improperly maintained or misadjusted commercial truck brakes can lead to tragedy when a truck needs to stop quickly.

Sometimes trucking companies will put a tractor-trailer back on the road soon after an accident. This damages the ability to have the condition of the brakes examined by a Texas truck accident attorney representing the victim. In a rear-end truck collision, the condition of the brakes may be the key to liability in your lawsuit against the trucking company. It is vital to contact a Texas truck accident lawyer as soon as possible after your wreck so that they may examine and test the condition of the brakes before any changes occur to the truck.

18 WHEELER TIRE BLOWOUTS

If you have driven on Texas highways, you have seen large chunks of shredded tires left by big rigs. These are the result of tire blowouts on big tractor-trailers which happen hundreds of times daily across Texas. The large tires used on commercial trucks are under high pressure and carry huge loads. This can cause the tire to violently explode under the right conditions and lead to deadly accidents that injure or kill surrounding drivers. Tire blowouts on 18-wheelers can hurl pieces through the windshield or even the metal body of nearby cars. A blowout of a front tire on a tractor-trailer can cause the truck to "jack-knife" where the tractor folds backwards along the trailer and the entire rig hurtles out of control. Tire failure on an 18 wheeler is usually caused by:

Poor maintenance

Defective tires

Failure to inspect the truck tires as required by federal regulations

Federal regulations require drivers to inspect tires daily to insure they are safe. In particular, drivers must look to see if tires are due for replacement or are underinflated (a leading cause of tire failure). When a truck driver fails to follow this inspection procedure it often leads to tragedy.

RETREAD TIRES

To save money, many trucking companies will use retreaded tires. These reconditioned tires are not a safe alternative in the trucking company's duty to keep their rigs safe. Federal regulations require the trucking company to keep the entire big-rig in safe condition, including the condition of the tires. The use of retreads to cut costs often leads to serious accidents when those tires fail and parts of the tire, or even the entire tire, fly down the road among passenger vehicles.

What special rules apply to commercial trucking companies?

FEDERAL REGULATION OF TRUCKING COMPANIES

Truck drivers and trucking companies are regulated by the **FEDERAL MOTOR CARRIER SAFETY REGULATIONS (FMCSR)**. The main regulations (FMCSR sections) which are important in many 18 wheeler lawsuits are:

391- **Qualification of drivers** - drivers must comply with this rule to be considered fit to drive commercial vehicles

392- **Driving of vehicles** – this rule covers pre-trip and post-trip inspections, the physical condition of the driver, etc.

393- **Equipment** - this rule covers vehicle condition and required safety equipment such as brakes, lighting and warning reflectors

395- **Driving time** - this rule outlines the maximum "on-duty" and driving hours a driver can log over a given period of time

The complete Federal Motor Carrier Safety Regulations can be found at **www.fmcsa.dot.gov**. With few exceptions, these rules apply to drivers and motor carrier companies which travel from state to state ("interstate" trucking companies). Many states including Texas have adopted these rules (with certain exceptions) to apply to the operation of commercial trucks within Texas ("intra-state" motor carrier companies).

What else can cause a tractor-trailer truck crash?

IMPROPERLY LOADED TRUCKS

Improper loading of a commercial truck is the cause of some Texas 18 wheeler accidents. Trucking regulations require that "no person shall drive a commercial motor vehicle and a motor carrier shall not require or permit a person to drive a commercial motor vehicle unless the commercial motor vehicle's cargo is properly distributed and adequately secured." Proper loading of a commercial vehicle insures that the load does not shift or fall off the truck during transport and that the load does not impede the driver's view. The regulations specify the steps the driver must take to insure that his cargo and equipment are properly loaded and secured. These steps include inspection of the load by the driver at the beginning of the trip and when a driver has driven for 3 hours or 150 miles or when the driver's "duty status" changes.

Many types of trailers are pulled behind big rigs. Flatbed trailers can be especially deadly in a wreck because the straps securing heavy items to the trailer can flex or break allowing items that may weigh more than a passenger car fall to off the trailer and strike innocent drivers.

What is the difference between "interstate" and "intrastate"?

INTERSTATE VS. INTRASTATE MOTOR CARRIERS

"Intrastate" in the context of a Texas trucking company means that a particular vehicle transports good only within the state of Texas. "Interstate" means that the truck carries goods between different states.

The difference between interstate and intrastate is important in a Texas truck crash. The truck must have the proper equipment and the proper load for the type of transport it performs. The tractor-trailer or other commercial vehicle must be insured for the correct type of transport in order for there to be insurance coverage available to pay for damages to the victims of a truck wreck.

What is a "Jackknife" accident?

JACKKNIFE ACCIDENTS

18 wheeler trucks are prone to a particular type of accident called a "jackknife". When the driver attempts to steer the truck with the "tractor" part of the big rig, the momentum of the "trailer" he or she is towing, especially when heavily loaded, may cause the trailer to continue in a

straight path while the cab folds sideways to the direction of the trailer. From the air, the result resembles a pocket knife or "jackknife" blade (the truck cab) being folded into the knife handle (the trailer). The result is that the driver is no longer in control of where the tractor-trailer goes and a serious accident usually follows.

Jackknife accidents may be caused by a front tire failure, road conditions, or faulty planning or reaction movements by the truck driver such as an attempt to change lanes or stop too quickly. Excessive steering input by a driver or a difference in speed or braking between the cab and the trailer are the usual causes of a jackknife. Onboard truck computers and accident reconstruction by an expert may be required to determine exactly what caused the jackknife accident.

What are the most common causes of truck accidents?

DRIVER ERROR

Many eighteen-wheeler truck accidents are avoidable. Although some accidents may be caused by equipment failure, many are caused by truck driver error. Poor planning, distraction and delayed reaction times by drivers can maim or kill other innocent drivers. Alcohol use, improper prescription drug use, illegal drug use, sleep deprivation, and distraction by using a cellular phone, computer or radio while driving can all lead to accidents.

Trucking company employee files, truck driver medical files, cellular phone and email records, driver log books and information from witnesses can help determine if driver error caused a Texas truck wreck. Enlisting the help of a Texas truck crash lawyer soon after your accident allows the attorney to gather this evidence to help you win your case before the evidence is lost or altered.

SPEEDING TRUCKS

While the average passenger vehicle weighs 3,000 pounds, 18 wheeler trucks can weigh up to 80,000 pounds. This fact places a special burden on big rig drivers to maintain control of their vehicle at all times and make safety their number one priority.

Unfortunately, the pressure on a driver to haul his load as far and as fast as possible may lead him to exceed the posted speed limit, or drive faster than is safe under certain traffic, road and weather conditions.

A tractor-trailer driver has the advantage of sitting high up, allowing a greater view than a typical passenger car of any potential traffic and road hazards ahead of the truck. However, as a rule of thumb it takes a semi-truck about one third longer to stop than a car or pickup truck. This makes driver reaction time and the speed of the commercial vehicle critically important. Add driver distraction to excessive speed and the result can be tragic. Rear end collisions, rollovers and jackknife accidents are often caused by excessive speed. Many commercial trucks today have an event data recorder or "black box" with a computer that saves data including speed of the truck prior to the crash. Finding this data and saving it as soon as possible after a Texas truck accident can be the key to proving driver negligence.

Where do most of the truck accidents in Austin and central Texas occur?

18 WHEELER ACCIDENTS ON INTERSTATE 35

Interstate Highway 35 stretches **1568 miles** from Laredo, Texas (near the Mexican border) to Duluth, Minnesota (near the Canadian border) and is the third-longest north-south highway in the United States. I-35 passes through the hearts of San Antonio, Austin and Dallas and carries hundreds of 18 wheelers and other commercial vehicles daily.

The section of I-35 between Austin and San Antonio (the "Austin-San Antonio I-35 corridor") is the busiest inter-metro interstate in Texas and carries over 100,000 vehicles daily. Many of these vehicles are large commercial trucks, and the number is rising with the rapid population growth of central Texas. The speed limit is 70 miles per hour along this entire corridor. But the speed limit is not always the safe speed, especially when your vehicle weighs 80,000 pounds and needs much more room to stop than a passenger car.

The high volume of tractor-trailers traveling at high speed through busy cities such as Austin and San Antonio often leads to accidents if truck drivers do not properly control their big rig or anticipate changing traffic, road or weather conditions and adjust their speed in time.

What type of insurance do truck companies have?

INSURANCE COVERAGE FOR TRUCK WRECKS

Because of the potential for serious injury and death, commercial trucks weighing more than 10,000 pounds are subject to regulation under the Federal Motor Carrier Safety Regulations are required to carry a minimum of $750,000 in insurance coverage. Many carriers choose to purchase a minimum of $1 million in liability insurance and many carriers with multiple trucks will carry an even larger "umbrella" insurance policy. Trucking companies that carry commercial passengers are required to carry greater amounts of insurance. Truckers that carry hazardous materials must have one million or five million dollars in insurance coverage depending on the type of material carried.

Lawyers and investigators for the truck company's insurance company will begin gathering evidence immediately after an accident to protect their financial interest by shifting the blame for the crash onto some other person, including the victim.

Insurance coverage issues in a commercial truck accident case can be complicated. To protect your rights and strengthen your claim, you need an attorney to begin gathering evidence favorable to your case as soon after the wreck as possible. An attorney can help insure that all available insurance is pursued to help you receive the largest recovery for your claim.

What are the other common types of truck accidents?

ROLLOVER ACCIDENTS

Commercial trucks carry huge loads. These loads usually ride high above the road. If a driver turns or changes lanes too quickly, the momentum of the load carried either in a "box" trailer or on a flatbed can force the entire truck to roll over on its side, crushing any nearby passenger cars and sending the entire tractor-trailer sliding down the highway out of control. It is vital that drivers anticipate necessary movements and control their speed to avoid rolling the truck.

"UNDER RIDE" ACCIDENTS

"Under ride" refers to a car going under the trailer of an 18 wheeler either from the side or the rear. This can occur when a truck stops too fast and the car goes underneath the rear of the truck. The flimsy barriers on the bottom rear of commercial trailers, which are designed to prevent this, often fold under the impact and allow the car to slide up under the truck.

Under ride can also occur when a car or truck changes lanes causing the car to go under the center of the trailer. Under ride can also occur if an out of control truck "jackknifed" big rig slides its trailer over the top of a passenger vehicle. Regardless of how it happens, the result is that hundreds of Americans are killed by under ride accidents every year.

When is a truck driver "negligent" in a crash and is the driver ever guilty of a crime?

NEGLIGENCE VS. CRIMINAL LIABILITY

Most 18 wheeler truck accidents in Texas are caused by negligence by the truck driver. Negligence means that the driver did not use the care expected of a professional driver of a large commercial vehicle to protect others on the road. This may include following too close, speeding, being distracted using a cellular phone, radio or computer, or simply not paying attention.

Sometimes, however, the actions of the driver warrant criminal charges and punitive damages in a civil lawsuit. Two examples are when a truck driver is intoxicated by either drugs or alcohol at the time of the accident. Falsifying the driver's log book to allow the driver to cover more miles than regulations allow can also be a criminal offense. Trucking companies may also be liable for punitive damages for allowing inexperienced or incompetent drivers behind the wheel or failing to properly maintain their trucks.

What exactly is a "personal injury case" anyway?

If you are in an automobile accident and the only thing injured is your car, you may have a property claim, but not a personal injury claim. If you are in an automobile accident and both you and your car are damaged, you may have both a property damage claim and a personal injury claim. If that is the case, usually your insurance company or the other party's insurance company will handle the property damage portion of your claim.

Not everyone who is injured in an accident has a claim against someone else. In order to have a legal claim regarding an injury, it needs to be the result of either someone else's intentional act or someone else's negligence.

If someone harmed you intentionally, you usually have a claim against them for any injuries you receive. You may also be able to have them charged with a crime. On the other hand, if you are injured by someone else who did not intend to harm you, the question is a little more complicated. You have to determine whether or not the other person's action was careless. **"Negligence"** is the legal term used to describe this carelessness. In general, negligence means that the other person failed to act the way a reasonably careful person would have acted in the same situation.

You also have to show that the other person had a duty not to act in the particular way that harmed you. You then must show that the other person breached that duty. You also must show that the action (or failure to act) of the other person actually caused your injury. Finally, you must prove what those injuries are, including past and future medical bills, past and future lost wages, and pain and suffering.

If a person is killed by the intentional act or the negligence of another, then that person, or their surviving family members, may have a "wrongful death" claim against the other party. Even in a wrongful death claim, the case needs to be evaluated to determine if anyone was legally at fault, or "negligent", for what happened.

Needless to say, the insurer for the trucking company will fight hard to prevent you from proving all these necessary parts of your case.

When discussing negligence, it is important to remember that it is usually a jury that decides whether or not someone was negligent when they injured you. Juries are made up of people, and people are unpredictable. Believe it or not, a jury could look at an accident where a truck rear-ended a car at a red light and decide that truck driver was not negligent under the circumstances, which means you would lose your case.

Particularly in this age of **"tort reform"** where the insurance industry has many spent many years and vast sums of money on a public relations campaign to convince the public that most personal injury claims are bogus, juries are often very reluctant to give much, if any, compensation to injured persons. Therefore, it is crucial that your case be presented as strongly and persuasively as possible.

You can never assume that your case is a "slam dunk" and that you will automatically win. Even an experienced personal injury lawyer cannot promise you what the outcome of your case will be if you go to trial (if any lawyer promises you a certain outcome at trial, you should get up and leave his office immediately). The point of this is that there are no "easy" personal injury cases. This is an important point to remember when evaluating, with the help of your attorney, the strengths and weaknesses of your case, the possible value of your case, and whether or not you should settle your case or take it trial.

What are the most common misconceptions about Texas truck crash cases?

The most common, **false** beliefs about commercial vehicle accident cases in Texas are:

* If I write the insurance company a nice, reasonable letter, I will receive a reasonable settlement offer.

* If I am in an accident, I always need an attorney.

* I should allow my lawyer to refer me to a doctor.

* If I am injured in an accident, and it was not my fault, there will always be an insurance company that will pay for my injuries, pain and suffering, and lost wages.

* If another person injures me, his insurance company is required to pay my medical bills as soon as they are incurred.

* When I have been an accident, the legal system is a way to get rich.

* If I am in an accident and the other person's insurance company requests a recorded statement, I must give one or they will not settle my case.

* The insurance adjuster is my friend.

* The main goal of the insurance company is to pay me fair compensation as soon as possible.

* Texas juries are generous.

What is the shocking reality of Texas truck wreck cases?

In theory, insurance companies provide a valuable service by spreading the risk we all face that we will be in an accident and incur expenses that we could not afford on our own. Insurance is a way for many people to pool their money to protect against the chance of one person (or a few people) incurring a large financial loss. In a perfect world, when you are injured in an accident, the insurance company would pay you a prompt, fair settlement for your injuries.

Unfortunately, the reality is different. Insurance is a business like any other. Their goal is to make a profit. The more premiums they collect, and the less they pay out in claims, the more money they make. This profit motive causes the insurance company to work very hard to pay you as little as possible (or nothing) for your injuries, regardless of who is at fault.

The insurance company (even your own insurance) is not your friend. They make money by collecting and investing premiums, not by paying claims. And, when you have been hurt by someone else, and you are trying to get the other person's insurance to pay for your injuries, the insurance company will fight you even harder. The insurance adjuster may discourage you from talking with an attorney. The adjuster may ask you to give a recorded statement, where you might say something that would damage your case.

Keep in mind that the insurance industry has spent many years and vast sums of money on two projects. First, they have conducted a vast public relations campaign to convince the public (from which juries are drawn) that most personal injury claims are bogus.

Second, insurance companies have spent a fortune and many years convincing lawmakers around the country to change the law to reduce or eliminate your ability to go to court to recover compensation when you are severely injured. Since the insurance industry is one of the richest in the country, and since it donates large sums of cash to political campaigns, the industry has been very effective in getting politicians to vote in their favor at the expense of the individual. Simply put, money talks, especially in politics.

As you fight the insurance company trying to get them to pay for your injuries you may have medical bills piling up. The insurance of the other person who injured you in your accident is usually under no obligation to pay your medical bills as they are incurred. This can cause severe financial hardship for many accident victims. This is one reason why it is important in serious accident cases to discuss your claim with an attorney as soon as possible. The attorney can evaluate your claim to determine if someone else was legally at fault, find out if there is insurance available to help pay for your injuries, and discover if there are any legal deadlines that must be met in order to avoid losing your ability to file suit on your claim.

What bad things can happen during my personal injury case?

The person at fault may not report the accident to their insurance company.

The insurance company may delay investigating the claim and accepting responsibility for the accident.

The person responsible for the accident may not have insurance coverage. If this is the case, you will have to file your injury claim with your own automobile insurance policy. If you do not have full coverage you may not be able to make any recovery. This is why every automobile owner should always add "Uninsured Motorist and Underinsured Motorist" (UM/UIM) protection coverage, as well as "personal injury protection" coverage (PIP) when the buy automobile insurance. UM/UIM helps repay costs that the other motorist's insurance (or lack thereof) cannot cover. PIP pays some of the out of pocket costs for medical treatment that you incur after an accident.

If are still paying off your car loan, and you fall behind on your payments because of medical expenses or missed work after an accident, the bank or the car dealership may repossess your car.

You may have paid too much for your car, including financing costs and the sales price. If this is the case, and your car is a total loss, you may be **"upside down"** on you loan. This means that the value of your vehicle is less than the amount of the loan that you still owe. In other words, you may end up without a car but still having to pay more money to pay off the loan. This also makes it very difficult to obtain another vehicle. To help protect against this there is a type of insurance coverage called **Guaranteed Auto Protection ("GAP") insurance** that he is good protection to consider buying if you buy a new car. It is also a good reason to search for the best deal on a car, including buying a used vehicle to avoid paying the new car "premium" that puts your finances at risk if you have an accident.

How do insurance companies and adjusters operate?

Usually, after an accident, while you are receiving treatment for your injuries, the party at fault in the accident will notify their insurance company. You also may contact your own insurance company in order to take advantage of any coverage they will need to provide, including the uninsured motorist protection (UM/UIM) and personal injury protection (PIP) coverage mentioned previously. The adjusters and investigators for the insurance company have lots of experience and they understand the importance of immediately investigating and processing accident claims.

Understand that the other person's insurance company has no obligation to inform you of your legal rights. All insurance companies employ very experienced adjusters and defense attorneys, who sole responsibility is to protect the financial interests of the insurance company. Insurance companies are mainly in business to make money, not to pay claims. The less they pay out in accident claims, the greater their profit.

Insurance adjusters are sometimes trained to take advantage of the lack of knowledge most claimants have about their legal rights and the value of their accident claim. The adjuster may seem like a nice person who is friendly and pleasant over the phone and seems concerned with your welfare. In fact, they might actually be a nice person. However, never forget that their primary job is to protect the insurance company. The way they protect the insurance company is by finding a way to not give you any money, or if they have to pay you money they want to make sure they pay you as little as possible in order to resolve the matter and make it go away.

When you talk to the adjuster, he or she may try to get you to minimize the impact or extent of your injuries, or to get you to accept some responsibility for the accident that was really not your fault. They may also tell you how difficult it would be for you win your case in court. These are all standard tricks of the insurance adjuster, and ones that an experienced attorney can help you avoid.

Recently, the American Bar Association published an article that shows that one large insurance company started a new program for training insurance adjusters. In this program, adjusters are encouraged to do whatever they can to speak to victims before they hire lawyers, including listening to police radios and visiting accident scenes.

When I have been injured in an accident, what should I do?

First, do not let anyone pressure you, threaten you, or intimidate you into making a quick decision or signing any type of document. It is very common for insurance adjuster to try to get you to sign away your rights quickly. If you do this, you will regret it later.

Second, document your injuries and the accident itself. Gather all medical records, accident reports, witness statements and contact information in a folder. Take photographs of the accident scene and your injuries as soon as possible and keep them with your file. As the old saying goes "a picture is worth a thousand words", and documenting your claim with photographs is worth thousands of dollars in helping you win a fair settlement or verdict for your accident.

Third, get as much information as you can about the personal injury claim process. Reading this guide is an excellent start. Discussing your case with an attorney that handles truck accidents on a regular basis and getting a "no obligation" evaluation of the strengths and weaknesses of your claim is also important.

Will I recover more money if I hire a lawyer than if I try to handle it myself?

Why do you think insurance companies engage in the outlandish behavior mentioned previously in order to get to injury victims before they hire an attorney? They are not doing it to help you. They are doing it to help their bottom line.

The Insurance Research Council conducted a study that found that injury victims that use lawyers in personal injury claims receive more money than those who do not use a lawyer, even after the attorney's fees are paid!

Insurance companies do not want you to hire a lawyer because they know they will end up paying more money for your claim. As I said before, insurance companies make profits by collecting premiums, not by paying claims. The less they pay you, the more profit they make. Insurance adjusters are not promoted or rewarded for paying out more money than they have to in claims, but by paying out less.

Many people every year do nothing, or accept much less money than they should, regarding their injury claim. Usually this is because these people do not know what to do after they have been injured, or they are led to believe that what they receive is all the money they can get. Many times, these injury victims feel confused or afraid. Do not let this happen to you! When you have been injured, doing nothing is the worst thing you can do.

What, then, should you do? Carefully review the following seven "fatal mistakes" that most accident victims make. Being aware of these mistakes will help you to avoid them, and usually will help you recover more money for your claim. This is important information that insurers hope you never find out!

What are the seven deadly mistakes that can wreck my Texas accident case?

Mistake # 1:

**Failing to take immediate action at the accident scene
to insure your rights**

After an accident you are usually shocked and confused and it is hard to make decisions. However, there are certain steps you should take immediately after the accident in order to protect yourself. Failure to do this could have serious consequences for your case. Remember that the following advice can apply to any type of injury case, not just truck accidents.

When you have an accident, stop your vehicle, but do not block traffic. Texas law prohibits you from leaving the scene of an accident, even if it is minor, until you first stop and see if there are damages or injuries. Remember to protect yourself. Do not immediately jump out of your car as you may be struck by oncoming traffic. If possible move the vehicles out of the lanes of traffic. If you're unable to move the vehicles out of traffic, warn other cars by setting out flares, turning on your hazard lights, and opening the trunk and hood of your car and any other vehicles involved.

Assist anyone is been injured, but if someone has a possible spinal injury, do not move them any more than absolutely necessary to get them out of immediate danger. Get the name, date of birth, phone number, address, driver's license number, license plate number and all other information of anyone else involved in the accident, including witnesses.

Do not argue with the other driver. Do not accuse anyone of being at fault, and do not admit fault. Stay calm. Remember that anything you say he can be used against you later. Do not discuss the accident with the other driver.

Call the police to come and complete an accident report. If it is an emergency, you can dial 911. If it is not an emergency, dial 311. Many times the other driver will try to talk you out of contacting the police. This is a mistake. Sometimes, the police will not come to the scene of a minor accident, but this is a decision you should let the police make. Be sure and call the police anyway, any time you are in an accident.

If an officer arrives at the scene, request that they make a written ask a report and ask them to give you the incident number for the accident so that you can get to report later, usually from the Texas

Department of Transportation records bureau. Get all information from the officer including his name and badge number and be sure and find out which police agency he is from (sheriff department, police department, Texas Department of Public Safety, etc.).

The police report should be available a few days after the wreck. Be sure and ask the officer where you can obtain the report. If you have an attorney, they will often get this report for you but if they do not, be sure and get it yourself. Once you get the report, review it very carefully to make sure all the details are correct. If there is a mistake in the report, contact the investigating officer and ask if they will be willing to correct the report. They will often do this if you notify them soon after the accident. Do not wait too long to request this correction, because the officer's memory of the accident will fade over time and he or she may be unwilling to change the report later.

If you were injured somehow other than in an automobile accident, for instance in place of business, demand to speak to the manager and insist that they make a written accident report. Also request that any video evidence, such as a security camera tape, that may show the accident be preserved. Preserving such evidence may be crucial to proving your case later

Be sure and write down the names, addresses phone numbers and license plate numbers of all witnesses to the accident, as well as all the parties involved. Pictures are very valuable in proving what happened at an accident scene. If you happen to have a cell phone that will take photographs, use it. If you do not have such a cell phone, it is a good idea to buy a cheap disposable camera to keep in the glove box of your vehicle, and use it to document any accidents as well as all of your injuries.

Remember to be safe, watching out for oncoming traffic. Take pictures of all the involved vehicles from different angles. Also photograph the street, including any stop signs and traffic signals. Also photograph skid marks and any other physical objects that may been damaged, such as telephone poles and guard rails. If possible, photograph the other drivers, witnesses and passengers. If you have been injured in are unable to take photos, please ask someone else to do it for you. If your cell phone is able to record video, that is useful as well in showing what happened at the scene.

It is a good idea to keep a pen and paper in the glove box of your vehicle. After an accident always exchange all your information with the other parties and get as much information as you can from the other persons, including their insurance information.

Do not make any statements regarding the accident except to the police or to emergency personnel such as EMS or fire department paramedics. If you feel unsafe or threatened at the scene of an accident, stay in your car with the doors locked until the police arrive.

Mistake # 2:

Not documenting everything that occurs after the accident

After an accident, it is important to document all the details immediately. If you wait, memories fade, wrecked vehicles are repaired or disposed of, witnesses move away, and other evidence becomes harder to locate. It is also helpful to keep a journal of your injuries and recovery, making a daily entry detailing pain, difficulty performing certain activities, what medications you had to take, and other difficulties caused by your accident. If you make these notes daily and include the date, they may be admissible to show, among other damages, pain and suffering, if your case goes to trial.

Mistake # 3:

Delaying visiting your doctor or not cooperating with your doctor

Seek medical treatment from a physician (M.D.) as soon as possible after your accident. Obtain and follow the recommendations for treatment from all the medical providers who treat you. Do not discontinue treatment until your physician advises you to do so. And do not take any "breaks" from your treatment - stay on the regular treatment schedule ordered by your doctor. Failure to do any of the above provides the insurance company and their lawyers the opportunity to argue that you were not really injured, or that your injuries were not very severe, or that you aggravated or prolonged your injuries by failing to follow the recommended treatment.

Mistake # 4:

Signing papers or giving statements without talking to a lawyer first

The insurance adjuster will usually ask you to give a statement of what happened and to describe your injuries. They may even offer you a settlement and ask you to sign a release. You should not do either of these until you review your case with an attorney. Otherwise, you might say something that damages your claim. Or, you might settle your case for less that the amount to which you are entitled if you do not know your rights and the strengths and weaknesses of your claim. Also, you might settle your case before you are completely healed, or before you know the full extent of your injuries.

Once you settle the case, you cannot return later and seek more money from the other party or their insurance, so you need to make sure you are receiving full and fair compensation for your injuries before you sign any release. You usually receive more compensation if you are represented by a competent personal injury attorney than if you try to do it yourself.

Mistake # 5:

Not hiring an attorney, or hiring the wrong one

If you have a "fender bender" with only property damage or some minor "soft tissue" damage, you may be able to settle it quickly and for a reasonable amount without using an attorney. However, if your injuries are more severe, or if your case is more complicated (which usually is true in commercial vehicle accidents) you will benefit from having an experienced attorney evaluate your claim and represent you.

Be sure that the attorney you consult with handles truck accident claims on a regular basis, and not just as a sideline to his or her many other practice areas. In today's complicated legal environment, it is difficult to be a "jack of all trades". If a lawyer handles cases from many different areas of law, it is difficult for him or her to be knowledgeable and up-to-date with the legal developments in all of those areas. And, it is hard for him to get sufficient experience in truck accident cases to develop good trial skills.

You would not want a specific type of surgery to be performed by a general practitioner who studied some surgery in medical school. In the same way, you need a trial lawyer who handles truck wrecks on a regular basis to handle you claim. The best leverage you have in trying to settle a claim with an insurance company is an attorney that has the ability to take the case to trial if necessary and who might win more than the insurer's settlement offer.

Mistake # 6:

Not being completely honest with your attorney, or failing to cooperate with your attorney

You must be completely honest with your attorney regarding what happened in your accident. You also must disclose any preexisting injuries, previous accidents, prior lawsuits, criminal history, drug and alcohol problems, work history and any other area of your past. Remember, in a truck crash injury lawsuit, the opposing attorney has the right to ask about any and all aspects of your past history, including your complete medical history. Therefore, you must disclose all of this information, especially the facts that you think might hurt your claim, so your attorney can evaluate them and work to limit any damage they might cause.

If your attorney knows about a problem with your past or with your case, he can work to limit the damage to your claim. However, if your lawyer is surprised by such information in a deposition or at trial, it can ruin your credibility and cause you to lose your case. If you lose the appearance of credibility with the insurance adjuster, the opposing attorney, the court or a jury, you will most likely lose your case. Besides, if something about your past or the facts of your claim will make your case difficult or impossible to win, you need to know that up front, before you and your lawyer spend lots of time and energy pursuing a losing claim.

Mistake # 7:

Exaggerating your injuries, or not being completely honest in any other way

As stated previously, credibility is absolutely essential if you hope to recover full compensation for your injuries. The best gift you can hand the opposing attorney is for you to lie or exaggerate your injuries. Once that happens, the case is usually lost. The best way to avoid this is to be completely honest, always. Be honest with your lawyer, be honest during depositions, be honest during settlement negotiations, and be honest during trial. That way, your story is always consistent and you never have to remember what you said before. Honesty also means admitting when you do not know or cannot remember something. There is no shame in not knowing all the details of every aspect of your case. Be honest and you will usually do fine in pursuing your claim.

What OTHER mistakes can destroy my truck accident case?

1.   **Waiting too long before seeking legal help.**

Texas law requires that you file your personal injury lawsuit within a certain amount of time after your injury. Otherwise, you will be prevented from ever filing a lawsuit on that claim. This is known as the **"statute of limitations"** for your claim. Your deadline can be affected by the details of your particular case. Also, if your claim involves any type of governmental entity (city, county, state, national) there are often much shorter deadlines with which you must comply. Waiting too long can be fatal to your case. Therefore, it is crucial that you contact an attorney as soon as possible to avoid missing these deadlines.

2.   **Hiding past accidents, injuries, job firings or lawsuits from your attorney.**

If you file a lawsuit regarding your injuries, the opposing party has a right to obtain all your past medical, accident and work history, as well as information on whether you have sued anyone or been sued by anybody before. Even if you do not give it to them voluntarily, they can probably obtain it from other sources, such as the insurance databases that all insurance companies subscribe to, court records or employee records. If you lie about any of these issues and get caught, your credibility is destroyed, and you will almost certainly lose your case. If you tell your attorney up front about all prior accidents, injuries, job firings, drug and alcohol problems, bankruptcies and lawsuits, he can evaluate whether or not it will be a problem for your current case. However, your attorney cannot deal with an issue about which he does not know.

It is particularly important that you be completely honest with your attorney regarding past injuries. If you saw a medical provider regarding that injury, there is a record that the insurance company will find. If you let your attorney know about a prior injury, he or she can evaluate it and deal with it. If you lie about it are later found out, your case is destroyed.

3. Getting a doctor referral from your attorney.

When juries find out that an attorney referred the client to a particular doctor, they become very suspicious of that relationship. The insurance company can find out how many times that attorney has referred patients to that particular doctor. A single referral raises suspicions. Multiple referrals confirm those suspicions. The only exception is if the client needs a very specialized type of medical care and the attorney steers them in the right direction. Make sure you understand the referral relationship between your attorney and that particular doctor before you accept any referral to that doctor. If an attorney pressures you to use a particular physician, you should avoid hiring that attorney.

4. Having inaccurate tax returns.

Most accident cases involve lost income. However, you can only claim and prove lost income if your tax returns are perfectly accurate. Also, lying on your tax returns could lead to more serious problems (criminal charges). Your attorney can help you deal with any potential problems in this area, but only if he knows about the problem beforehand.

5. Misrepresenting your activity level

Believe it or not, insurance companies regularly hire private investigators to conduct videotape surveillance of injured claimants. If you claim you cannot do a certain activity, and you are caught on videotape doing it, your claim is over. The key here, as in the rest of your personal injury claim, is to never exaggerate, either to your attorney, the insurance company, a judge or a jury. Honest, injured people can still obtain good results in court, but liars lose.

6. Exaggerating your injuries

To be successful in a truck accident claim, you need to be totally honest. This is particularly true in today's climate, where many jurors are suspicious of personal injury plaintiffs to begin with. If you exaggerate your injuries, the other side (and the jury) will usually find out. Once this happens, they can portray you as a liar and your credibility is ruined. You must be honest with your attorney from the very beginning regarding the circumstances surrounding your accident, your previous accident history, your previous medical history (including any prior injuries), your previous work history (including reprimands and firings), your previous involvement in lawsuits, and all other aspects of you and your background. If your attorney knows about any potential problems ahead of time, he can deal with it. But he can only deal with the problems about which he knows.

7. Not working with your attorney as a team

Although the attorney is in charge of preparing the case, he or she will need your help to do so. During the course of a personal injury case, it is essential that your attorney be able to contact you and, when necessary, enlist your help in obtaining certain information and documents. You will also need to be available to assist your attorney by answering discovery requests (formal, written requests for information) from the other side, preparing for depositions and preparing for trial. The best attorney in the world cannot help you if you do not assist him in preparing your case.

Remember that when you go to trial, you are **"Exhibit A"**. If the jury does not like you and does not believe you, they will look for a way to deny you what you are requesting, and you will lose. The way to be likable and believable is to assist your attorney in preparing ahead of time for your testimony, being completely honest at all times and being courteous to everyone involved in the case, including the opposing attorney. If the jury likes you and believes your story, they will usually try to find a way to help you recover for your injuries.

What automobile insurance definitions should I know?

It is important that you understand the basics of automobile insurance coverage when dealing with a truck accident. The following definitions should be helpful to you.

Bodily injury liability

This type of insurance requires that your insurance company pay the claim to a person who is injured because of your carelessness or the carelessness of some driving your car. However, the insurance company is only liable up to the amount of coverage you bought. For example, if you bought the Texas minimum liability limits of $30,000.00 per person and $60,000.00 per accident for injuries, and $25,000 for property damage (often written in insurance shorthand as "30/60") and you are at fault in an accident, your company will pay no more than $30,000.00 to each injured person and no more than $60,000.00 total for injuries from any one accident. You would be personally liable for any damages above those insurance coverage amounts.

Property damage liability

This type of coverage is similar to the bodily injury liability coverage discussed above, except that it covers damage to another person's property and not physical injuries. As with bodily injury liability, insurance companies only obligated to pay up to the amount of coverage you bought. The minimum limit for this type of coverage in Texas is $25,000.00. Obviously,

$25,000.00 is often not enough money to repair a badly damaged the vehicle in this day and age, so I recommend that you purchase additional coverage, which can be surprisingly inexpensive.

Comprehensive

This type of insurance requires the insurance company to pay you for damage to your car caused by something other than an auto accident (for example, theft, vandalism or fire). The company's obligation is reduced by the amount of "deductible" you purchased. If your deductible is $500.00 that means you pay the first $500.00 in damage and the insurance company pays the rest.

Collision

This coverage requires that your insurance company pay you for damage to your car caused by an automobile accident. Again, the amount your insurance company must pay is reduced by the amount of deductible you purchased.

Personal injury protection

This type of insurance coverage (PIP) pays the reasonable medical expenses of anyone in your car who is injured in an accident, regardless of who was at fault. You and most members of your household do not even have to be in a vehicle for this coverage to apply. For example, if you are struck by a car while you are walking, you would still be covered. This coverage can also repay you a portion of your lost earnings. Of course, as with any insurance, the amount the insurance company must pay is limited by the amount of coverage you purchase. In Texas, you can purchase personal injury protection in amounts of $2,500.00 (the minimum unless your reject this coverage in writing), $5,000.00, and $10,000.00. I recommend that you purchase as much of this coverage is you can afford, because it is cheap insurance and is very useful if you're involved in an accident.

Uninsured motorist

If you or the other occupants of your car are injured by an uninsured driver this coverage (UM) will pay for physical injuries. This coverage substitutes for bodily injury liability insurance that the other driver should have had, but did not. Again, this coverage is limited by the amount of insurance you buy. The minimums in Texas "per person/per incident/property damage per accident" are the same "30/60/25" as discussed above, unless you reject this coverage in writing. Also, like personal injury protection, this coverage applies whether you are a pedestrian or whether you are an occupant of a vehicle.

Underinsured motorist

If you or the other occupants of your car are injured by a driver whose liability insurance is insufficient to cover the full value of your physical injury claims, this insurance (UIM) will make up the difference. As always, the insurance company's obligation is limited by how much coverage you purchased. And, as with uninsured motorist and personal injury protection, this coverage is not limited to occupants of automobiles.

How can I win the "insurance war"?

You should not be shy about asserting your right to be compensated for your injuries caused by someone else. After all, just like everyone else who purchases insurance, you paid in advance so you will be able to recover your losses if you get hurt. So it may sound strange when I tell you that from the moment you were injured by someone else's carelessness, you entered a war zone. Why do I refer to this situation as a **"war zone"**? This is a war because in the last few years insurance companies and many government officials have worked very hard and spent vast sums of money in order to limit the ability of injured Texans to recover fair compensation when they are injured. This is a war to deprive you of your ability to recover your rightful compensation when you have been injured.

This campaign has been sold under the name **"Tort Reform".** The tort reformers claim that their goal is to lower insurance rates for individuals and decrease the cost of doing business. In reality, it is a cynical effort to increase the bottom line of the insurance industry and to help businesses avoid liability when they injure their employees or the public. If you don't believe it, ask yourself: "Have my overall insurance rates decreased since the start of tort reform?" The answer for most people is a resounding "No!" Also, talk to any one of the thousands of people who have been mistreated by the insurance industry after an accident and see if they think tort reform has helped their situation.

You should also know that the tort reform advocates succeeded in imposing **"caps"** that limit damage amounts that may be awarded in certain types of personal injury cases. This means that much of the decision of how much to compensate you when you have been injured by someone else has been taken away from juries and placed in the hands of your legislature. The Texas legislature has "capped" damages without regard to the individual circumstances of different cases.

For example, if you collide with your physician on the freeway, he can sue you and recover millions, depending on his injuries.

However, if that same physician maims or kills you through his negligence during surgery, you can only recover $250,000.00 worth of noneconomic damages (pain and suffering) under most circumstances. If you are a child, a nonworking housewife or a retired elderly person, you usually cannot claim any lost income, so this will probably be all the compensation you can ever recover from the doctor or hospital that injured you. Does that seem fair to you?

Since insurers know that, thanks to "tort reform", it is now much harder for you to recover compensation through the courts, they have even less incentive to offer you a reasonable settlement.

Regardless of how you feel about tort reform, it is important to remember that the vast insurance industry propaganda media campaign regarding tort reform has strongly influenced potential jurors. When you walk into a courtroom in Texas, you must understand that many jurors will assume upfront that your lawsuit is frivolous (think the "McDonald's coffee case") and that you're trying to "get rich quick". So even if you believe that there are many "frivolous lawsuits" and that yours is one of the rare legitimate cases, you are already at a disadvantage in the mind of your jurors.

Knowing this, insurance companies will usually not offer a fair settlement unless you are ready, willing and able to go to trial. Think about it. The only thing that forces an insurance company to take your claim seriously is the threat that you might file a lawsuit, take them to court and win more money than they offer to settle.

This also highlights why it is very dangerous to trust your case to an attorney that runs a "settlement mill", meaning they take too many cases, hope to settle all of them, and never take anything to trial. If they are forced to take something to trial, they "farm the case out" to a trial attorney. The insurers know which attorneys take cases to trial. If the insurance company knows that your attorney never takes anything to trial, they will not take your claim seriously and will not offer you anything reasonable in settlement. Also, if your case does need to go to trial, wouldn't you rather start out with an attorney that is ready, willing and able to try your case?

What if I am partially at fault for my accident?

Understand that in Texas the law of **"comparative negligence"** controls how much money, if any, you can recover from someone who causes your injury. If the jury finds that you were partially at fault for the accident, they will reduce the amount you recover by the amount you were at fault. If the jury finds you were more than half at fault for your injuries, you will recover nothing.

For example, if your damages total $100,000.00 and if a jury awards you that amount but determines that you were 20% at fault, your $100,000.00 would be reduced by 20%, or $20,000.00, leaving you with $80,000.00. If the jury finds that you were more than 50% at fault in your accident, you will recover nothing. It may not seem fair, but it is the law in Texas.

Do I need an attorney at all?

Not every case needs an attorney. Many small injury cases can be settled directly with the insurance company. Sometimes, it makes more sense to settle a small case without the help of an attorney because attorney's fees and other costs, including your medical bills, might leave little or no compensation for you when the case is finished. This is especially true of a **"fender bender"** with some minor property damage and perhaps some minor **"soft tissue"** physical injuries, like a sore neck or sore back that clears up in a few days.

On the other hand, if your case involves serious injuries or complicated issues of who is at fault it becomes more important to have an attorney working on your side, or to at least to consult with an attorney prior to talking to the opposing party or the insurance company. Because they usually involve serious injury, if you are in a commercial truck accident you should discuss your situation with a Texas truck accident lawyer as soon as possible.

Do I ever have to pay back the medical bills that were paid by my own insurance company?

Believe it or not, the answer is usually **"yes"**. Health insurance policies often require you to repay your own insurance company or your employer's health plan at least some of the money they spent for your medical care, using any money that you recover in your personal injury case to do so. This is true of Medicare and Medicaid as well. It is important that you review with your attorney the terms of your own insurance policy to see if you're required to repay any of these costs and whether you can negotiate a lower repayment amount with your insurer. This right of your insurance company to recover their costs from your settlement or verdict, known as **"subrogation",** is a complicated area of law. You should discuss this issue with your attorney as soon as possible after your accident.

What about trying to settle the case without filing a lawsuit?

Sometimes a case can be settled without filing a lawsuit. Remember, however, that all personal injury lawsuits and Texas are governed by a **"statute of limitations"**. This means that if you do not file a lawsuit on your injury claim within a certain period of time, you can never file suit on that claim. It is extremely dangerous to wait until you get close to the end of your statute of limitations in order to file a lawsuit, because you lose valuable preparation time and the opportunity to discover if there are any problems with your case, or if there are other parties that should be included in the suit before time runs out.

There are attorneys that routinely wait until the last minute to see if the insurance company will settle the case. If a settlement does not happen, these attorneys panic and race to find someone to file suit on the case, or they withdraw as the attorney and force the victim to find a trial lawyer to help them at the last second.

Why Did I Write This Guide?

I wrote this book because many people who have been injured in truck accidents in Texas make mistakes that damage their case, Usually due to a lack of good information on how to protect their rights. I believe the information in this book will help protect you from the pressure and scare tactics used by many insurance companies, and some attorneys, against accident victims. When truck accident victims are better informed they make better decisions regarding their case.

About David Todd

Texas Truck Accident Lawyer David Todd is devoted to helping victims of 18-wheeler and other commercial motor vehicle accidents. Learn more at **davidtoddlaw.com.**

David Todd, Attorney at Law
Todd Law Firm
3800 N. Lamar Blvd., Ste. 200
Austin, TX 78756
(512) 472-7799
davidtoddlaw.com

www.ingramcontent.com/pod-product-compliance
Lightning Source LLC
Chambersburg PA
CBHW021504210526
45463CB00002B/889